Why I'm Unable to Earn a Living….
We weren't meant to survive because it's all a set-up!

By

Angela C. Williams

Why I'm Unable to Earn a Living…
We weren't meant to survive because it's all a set-up!

By

Angela C. Williams

Copyright© 2015
ISBN-13: 9781518746369
ISBN-10: 1518746365

Dedication
To my beautiful daughter Indigo Skye

Introduction

Although there is a Black male on the cover, I am very much, a Black woman. How is it even possible that I have a college degree, a trade license for Cosmetology, and 13 books, all written by me; and I do not even have one dollar in my pocket or in the bank. Did I fall and bump my head? What's your guess? I really don't think I've made that many mistakes in life; over and over again. It's clearly a conspiracy. The reason definitely shouldn't be that I've slept with too many men before I really got to know them. I only have one child. And she is by my ex-husband. I know; you're looking at the cover of one of my other books, and thinking; "Well, she's really not that good looking, she doesn't have big breast-and she's dark-skinned too." But other than a slight little hump in the bridge of my nose, I think I'm quite attractive. Especially when I smile. (I look a lot younger than my age; believe it or not).

I can't work because the entire world believes the TV and movie lies about me. I'm truly not a cheater or a liar. The entire world is pretending that they didn't leave me homeless, forcing me to seek shelter with strangers. Male strangers. Everyone believes that I'm the young woman in the TV show *How To Get Away With Murder*. The one having sex in the laundry room during season 2. I've had sex in a laundry room before but I was being intimidated during my homeless situation by a man who I believed was my boyfriend. I would never seduce a man and/or strip down and say "you don't want this". By the way. The way to get away with murder is to leave a relative whose just lost his or her job, outside without a financial savings or shelter.

Yup, it's true. I have no female friends and no man in my life. They all believe that I smell like (the Jordan character)in the movie The Best Man. They also believe I'm Mia, the character who is being sexed from behind just because she "wanted it". I'm quite sure this is one of the main reasons why I'm harassed when I'm at work; even though my last name is no longer Harper. I've never been studying with anyone and then began making out with them. That movie was made a long time ago. That's how long every man has been believing it. They are all married now, to the people who the movie is really portraying. I'm still single and friendless. No I did not sleep with anyone in my ex-husbands wedding party. It's no wonder that every human male thinks of me when they see a sex scene. The woman in sex scene in Bad Boys is dark brown, as well as the woman in The Best Man.

Everyone thinks I've had sex with googobs of men 'and it's all been televised'. But just for an example: Me and Duane levy were a couple briefly in high school. If you ask him, we had sex. If you ask me, we didn't. I think he is very attractive and we were close friends for a long time. He and I had been friends since our summer league track team during middle school. Our parents even grew up in the same town. The ONE time that we were supposed to have had sex (at his home, during high school) it didn't happen. Why didn't we have sex again? And why didn't he invite me to the prom? No, I did not smell. I didn't have sex on prom night. I love him to this day and I'm not saying this to be mean. Was it just a quest to say he slept with me; as it may have been for many others? I guess you can say one reason why I'm unable to work is because it took me too long to realize that apparently Black men have sex with all of the easy women they can possibly find before they decide to settle down and transfer all of their acquired diseases to a woman who plays hard to get, before he marries her.

I'm sure that now many who have read my two books that speak of my years in grade school, think I was having some sort of relationship with my Physics teacher because I said I went to the prom alone but danced with him when I arrived. He was a great teacher. I liked Physics and I learned a lot. I worked hard in his class as well as the others. He never made a pass at me. He never spoke inappropriately.

Recently, I've been watching the new TV series, How to Get away With Murder. Let me tell you how you TRULY get away with murder. Write a real life character into every Hollywood movie script. Include two small innocent, true facts about her life. Then incorporate two large lies into that specific story. Do that for 2 decades. Then leave her homeless after harassing her from her job of 7 years. That's how you get away with murder. Oh OK...

I never had a chance in any relationship, from the beginning; with men, or female friends; after my divorce. Notice in the movie Double Jeopardy that my name is used as the bad person.

My husband and I had a gas leak when we lived on Hallam Ct. I called BG&E at least three separate times. Each time they found a leak. It was never fixed. During this time my husband grabbed me violently, immediately before we entered the church building because I was crying and he didn't understand why. After that incident with my husband; my ex; or my first love, and I became intimate twice. I then told my husband and I left for good. " Angela, how long have you been sleeping with my husband?" *Double Jeopardy*. This was blatant sabotage. My family and even my closest of friends at that time, believed it. I am still friendless to this day. No wonder no one wanted me to spend the night in their home when I was left homeless by my father and extended *family*.

(You know. None of us want to live next door to a sexual predator right. Why don't we harass them off of their jobs so that they can't afford a home wherever they choose to live. Then, they will be forced to live in the woods next to our children's schools.)

How can I work, when all things sane tell me that the slow jams on the radio years ago were from my ex-husband; ('come home Charlene') and from some ex- boyfriends. And I also believe that movies like High School Musical, are my female girlfriends telling me to wise up. (And no I never slept with any ballplayers in high school or college; except my husband.) Why wouldn't they just talk to me instead of forcing me to socialize solely, with gorgeous, smoking , drinking ex-cons who they all knew, were already *Taken*.

Now, the fact that I was set-up straight out of high school is an important factor regarding the reasons why I'm unable to work. I'd never had sex in a car or even made out in a car until after I met my soon to be husband in college. He and I made out and that's it. I actually didn't have sex in a car until after my husband and I separated. I have never robbed any stores and no one almost raped me during my high school years. I never had sex in any hotels until I became homeless. And it wasn't for money. Now that I've watched Thelma and Louise for the first time (November - 2015), the producers and actors interject a statement of; "No, it's too late for you to say this stuff isn't true". Lil Kim, Angie Mar and company told you way back then that, I suppose; my brother and I, would have to get our money by stealing; they just beat around the bush a little. Well, we don't steal. And I'm not gonna live my life on the run. But clearly we're being set-up. I wasn't a ho then and in spite of the entire world working against me to justify violating my civil rights and forcing me to befriend ex-convicts; (able to only have, literally one friend at a time; except for woman), I refuse to sell sex or marry the first penis that comes along, in order to have shelter and food. How does a woman escape being raped by a drunk stranger, then a few days later, have sex with a random man on a road trip? (Geena Davis-Thelma and Louise). Susan Serandan sits on the floor and says, "No this is not Ok". No, not having any money, is not OK. (I went to prom alone and I didn't have sex at the hotel party afterwards). Yes Prince, me and my (inseparable) best friend in High School, wore peach T- shirts with black shorts on the very first day and my neighbor and school mate with the last name Hudson, was really taken a back that we had done so. I'd gotten my hair done every two weeks since the age of 5 until I left for college, and a really flamboyant, woman sporting personalized tags on her red corvette, was a stylist there. I'm willing to bet my pinky finger, that if this story is actually true about these two women on the run; that it's White folks; but ever since it was

made and that Thelma and Louise rap song by Black people;
"we" have been made to look like the culprits.' My brother
was set-up. And I'm not a ho. My life-long male friends
believed this shit. Excuse my French. They chose to never take
me serious in relationships because of it. But I didn't know
that. And Prince, by the way, neither me nor Nicky, wore
make-up. We rarely wear it now.

Thank you Obama for not having me arrested or put in jail for
pan-handling to sustain shelter and food for my daughter and
myself. Thank You. Please help me.

Just recollecting while waiting to be helped.....

Yes, Timothy, I had sex with you in your car after my
separation from my husband in 1997. I did not know then,
that it was against the law. (No one could see us). I've known
you forever; I loved you, I trusted you and I'd never had sex
in a car before. And yes I believed we were in a relationship.
Although *Bad Boys,* the movie; made everyone believe it was
wild and 'ronchy'; it wasn't. Timothy lived in North Carolina
and I lived here with my parents. Why does everyone feel the
need to know when I have sex-(even when it's somebody
else)? Yes I kissed my ex in a car before I left my husband. No
he didn't walk up to the car and say, "What did I do?"(Will
Smith). He didn't need to; because for no reason at all, he had
already put his hands on me. He nor anyone else, caught me
in a compromising position. I told him what I did and then I
left my marriage. I would never start a new relationship
unless the current one was already over.

Let me ask you another question. Did you notice the Cressida
vehicle 'pan to' shot in Hitch or the the 'out of control '
argument scene outside of the home with Saban, in

Love Jones? Well. I've stood on the steps of Columbia University and I do look a lot like that young woman asking for directions; and I married a man who wore the same shirt as Will Smith as he speaks to her; in Hitch - and I do have a cousin who looks even more like that female actor than I do and she happens to have had a boyfriend named Alex; but I have never had an argument, in the front of our home; with my husband. My parents didn't yell at us and we didn't raise our voices at them. (Nor did they yell at each other). Our family "seemed perfect". TV tried their 'damndest' to discredit us all. Jesus help us.

Make no mistake about it; those Black, White, Asian, African and Hispanics; regardless of financial or professional status, who have watched countless movies over the years and believe they are seeing me having sex; are whore-minded and obsessed. Those reading my books and believe that what I'm saying, implicates me as a 'ho'; are ghetto, narrow-minded and not very smart. I am not bi-polar and I do not do drugs. There has never been a time in my life where I have drank too much and found myself in a compromising position with any male. I've never been in a bedroom of a party with a male, kissing or touching or drinking.

You know when I mentioned oral sex in my first book of poetry, there are tons of folks who automatically think, money and/or strangers. It baffles me how Blacks are quick to say I've been used for sex. They all left me homeless on purpose. I do not feel that I have ever been used. See when I say I'm 'open' for something, I mean, I will consider the idea seriously. See, to say, that vienna (sausages) waits for you; is beside the point I'm making in my books. The ENTIRE WORLD believes what they have seen or heard about me. I made friends with those who to me were friendly. Not caring that my female friends abandoned me. I didn't become physical at all with the majority of the men I made friends with. Friends, not clients.

There are numerous reasons why Black people in general are unable to find and or maintain employment; but today I will be focusing on myself. I do not fit the typical outline of those in the welfare office or those living in the lower income part of the inner city. I truly don't share their philosophy or outlook on life, either (well, not a lot of them). I must say that I have a greater understanding and sympathy for the Black man who was raised by a struggling Black woman. I have a greater respect for Black youth who did not have parents who aimed for higher education. However, I do not understand why Black youth do not put forth the best effort possible to pay attention in class; read, study and focus on changing the path of their family's history. However, I guess if you don't know that you need to wear glasses or your parents can't afford them, then passing tests could be challenging. If you have a history of Bi-polar behavior in your family, or bipolar depression, but you are unaware; that could be another reason why you may not be able to focus and study properly. To my Black brothers in jail or finally out; I do not know the feeling of such helplessness, especially if you are innocent; however, although I am unable to study an become an attorney, I will write every book and letter possible, and even try to make a film to explain the lack of justice that you withstand and sometimes, succomb to. (I do not believe that people who commit non-violent crimes, should have to go to jail). I have never lived in an environment where, peer pressure, violence, or drugs and alcohol, played a major role in my immediate surroundings. And for that, I must give honor to my parents and grandparents. (And of course to my Lord and Savior.) But I thank God for the young woman who listened to the voice of God; I would say it was, when she invited me to be a part of the Boys and Girls Club at age 9. I only wish that myself or someone else, had invited my brother, as well. I want to say I was lucky to attend a high school in a more affluent area and that's why I was able to focus on my academics; but, my daughter attended the same high school as my former girlfriend who is now a brain surgeon-(and that school was not in a very affluent area). I know that my daughter should be able to reach her goals if she puts forth the effort and learns from my mistakes. She will just have to watch out for pitfalls like the one I endured at a tennis tournament that I attended in Virginia Beach with a man that my cousin set me up with. A guy at our dinner table handed me a pill. I took a pill thinking it was for my headache. It was an illegal drug. I could tell something wasn't right by my insane behavior after I took it. I was walking really fast. I've never done drugs. I plan to write several more books that maybe one day will make for a great movie. I say that, because clearly society doesn't think that they should support my writing. At least not right now. I mean I know people don't really read books, like they read the newspaper or a magazine, but, what I'm dealing with is definitely worth noting for history sake. I believe.

I think you should ask yourself, "How can I be angry that crime is surmounting all across the globe", if you are not an intricate part of the plan to hire ex-convicts when they are released into society. Are you helping your juvenile delinquent child find a legal way to make money? I'm guessing that many of you parents will say that your child is too far gone and you can not reach him or her. I can relate, somewhat. I lost the connection with my daughter when she and I were left homeless and we were separated by our family. I'm still not back on my feet so she doesn't want to hear anything I have to say.

Maybe later on in life she will read this and understand that it truly wasn't me. I'm being set up. I was offered 4 different jobs from 4 large companies while I was homeless. Either they didn't' want to pay me more than $7.35 an hour working part-time or they wanted me to travel on three buses one way at 5:am for apart-time position, or I was working with men who were intimidated that I was really a serious sales person and may end up 'taking their potential sales' as they put it. When none of the following were the issue, someone smelly or not, was lying and saying that I smelled when I truly didn't. I couldn't pay for a room or our hotel making $7.35/hr. Panhandling always ended up being my means of paying for everything.

The Meat of the Book
(Please keep in mind. These are real reasons why I am unable to earn a living.)

Point 1

I wanted to give my daughter a life parallel to that in which I'd experienced but I was clearly unable to do so. I'm happy to see that she is able to make and keep friends in the midst of all of the trials she and I have faced. She lost the friendship of the children of those suburban friends that I'd grown up with and now has friends whose parents know what it's like to struggle. I managed to live for roughly 35 years without having to go before a judge as a criminal of the law. What's my crime you ask? Calling a Black man too many times in a row. I didn't end up in jail but I did get probation before judgement or something like that. I was sentenced to community service. Absolutely unbelievable. I had just been left homeless too. I knew him years prior. Well anyway. This was the first reason why finding employment was challenging. At least until I had the record expunged three years later.

I know that part of the reason why it's difficult for me to find employment is because I've been in this area for a long time and I left several decent paying jobs with the intent to work for myself in my trade. I should have done both until I'd solidified a strong clientele base. I just really hated one of the jobs and the other, well, I was disappointed that a few of the relationships I'd attempted to sustain, (within the company) ended in the entire company thinking I was a ho. I didn't really feel like people thought I was a ho. I was embraced at the Christmas party. And never really verbally harassed. But I was truly disappointed. And at the time, unable to separate the two and hold on to a thriving career. I wasn't being a ho. I didn't even know then, that people thought I sucked his dick to get promoted. Meanwhile, back at the ranch…

Those writers in Hollywood California must have been watching and thought it would be a good idea for the world to know about my ordeal at this particular company. They somehow found a way to infuse a little bit of information regarding this matter, into almost every movie released. It has yet to cease. Check out my Libel and Slander Book and you will see exactly what I mean. One of the guys actually came to me years later and said, "My God, you're never gonna get over it". He couldn't believe it either. This was the guy who'd pressed charging against me. I knew he was married then, but I thought he was getting a divorce. Anyway.

Point 2

When I left for college, me and my friends, all went in different directions. They all seemed to be heading south. I went North. That shouldn't break up life-long friendships. After being left virtuously friendless by females; including my Christian Sorors from my college days, And being bombarded by potential male relationships that did not result in sex; I was introduced to my future husband by his football teammate, and our mutual friend at the time.

I suppose I should ask myself why I got married so soon out of college. But I don't really need to. It was to honor God. Unfortunately it was a real-life, major set-up. No friends, and being bombarded by guys. After leaving to play on the practice squad of the Washington Redskins and being cut; my future husband; moved back in with his parents. They were pastors and had just moved into a house on Mary Ridge Drive in Baltimore County. Until many years later, neither me nor my mother watched soap operas. I wonder who it was who recommend that my mother begin watching The Young and The Restless? When I returned home after my separation, I began watching it as well. I suppose I was Brook and now they are 'over me'. Over-Brook Productions. I never showed any interest in his father.

Point 3

My mother was diagnosed with cancer. She died in the house, right in front of me. Pancreas cancer. She and my father always did everything together. They even worked at the same place. I suppose she must have been telling everyone except me, that she wanted me to leave work and go with her to the hospital. I didn't always know when she had appointments but I knew my father was driving her everywhere. He always went with her. Somehow she drove herself to work each day but she said it kept her mid sane. She wanted to keep her daily routine going so she wouldn't just think about being sick. From my understanding, the people at her job, could see how much pain she was in. it didn't realize that they were trying to get me and her to leave work, to spend tie together. They just kept verbally harassing both of us. Why couldn't they just be normal so she would not think about being sick? That's what she wanted. It's not rocket science but it does take focus to cut and color effectively. Constant harassment makes it extremely hard to work on any job. I wasn't then, and nor am I now, paranoid. I ended up losing my largest clientele and she was being hurt and harassed, her last days at work.

During this time I had the copyright for my first poetry book processed. The misinterpretation of one of my poems, as me being bitter and the introduction of such poetry into the Hollywood movie scripts, gave a false impression of my true character. Example: I'm severely allergic to shelled fish and one of my poems reads- A Noun or a Verb. Checkout the movie Hitch.

I will not be able to work because everyone believes I was interacting inappropriately with my ex- boyfriend when I first got married. When in actuality, my husband was violent with me out of the blue just because I was crying and said I wasn't happy on our way to church. That in-turn lead me talk to my ex-boyfriend inappropriately. Everyone relates the movie Soul-Food to me.

They all wanted the roof scene with the loose, dancing cousin, to become me. It took 17 years but they finally made it happen. They separated me from my daughter and left me outside without a job. Forced me to move to Philly with my cousin and her new husband in order to have a place to sleep. I don't have casual sex. They thought I was willing to share. I thought their marriage was over. So all of the desperate house-wives in my family from both sides, got their wish. Anyway. I thought I had a decent family. Guess I was wrong.

The movie Barber Shop had just come out. I guess they all thought I was Eve. My aunt Terry stopped by to visit me while I was at the salon and my parents brought me flowers for my birthday. "You're not that cute, it's just that thing you do"-a line from the movie script. I'm not a robot. And I'm grown. Why sabotage my career, Hollywood. Unnecessary and crazy is what it was. The movie had already been released. They set me up to be mad at my mother. I have never cursed at any employees or clients or in the presence of either in any hair salon. I have never cursed in the presence of customers in any retail environment. When did curse at the Human Resources man at the Wal-mart where I intended on quitting and stated so, right after I cursed him out. Then he in-turn, said,"You're fired". The idea is to make the records show that I keep being fired from jobs that I acquire. I am extremely professional. I am not violent and I do not talk nasty to customers.

I worked as a substitute teacher for almost seven years after that- (2002-2009). Although I had attended Graduate school briefly to take courses that would help me be more effectively in the classroom. I was compensated well in my current long term subbing positions and I figured layoffs would happen to teachers before substitutes. I wasn't too distraught with the discovery that I hadn't passed the math section of the Praxis Exam. The entire time I was there, I was vigorously harassed by students. They called me a "ho". I had no idea what they were talking about. They proceeded to blurt out personal information that was not completely true but way too personal to be repeated. They were not successful in ending my teaching career that way, so the; (probably along with their parents); concocted a scheme to start a physical fight with me. Sixteen years of schooling and 30 odd years of life and I'd managed to not be in any physical altercations. Long story short-Two male students struck me from behind while fighting in the classroom. As a reflex, I smacked one on the arm. I lost my job with the Prince George's County School System. I then became 'homeless' with a young, school-aged daughter. I was not evicted. I'd left my apartment and moved in with family before I lost the job.

Point 4

I was intentionally forced to pan-handle so that 'criminals' could prove that after a charge, you will not be able to find work. This was done to me while we had a Black president. Every Black man and woman was more than happy to give me money as I stood on the median with my homeless sign. After going before the judge again for pan-handling and getting community service, I began walking around in parking lots all across the region, asking for money. (This must have been a part of their plan). I paid for our hotel this way; for years until my daughter graduated from high school. I guess that's why she hates me. I tried to work. She thinks I can't work because I was too easy and now the world is harassing me and calling me a ho. If I complained, then they would have the audacity to say stuff like-" You think something is wrong with us? We aren't the ones walking around in the parking lot asking for money." No, they're just the ones harassing me off of certain jobs, sabotaging me on the other ones and refusing to get their hair done or buy my books.

Since I've been left homeless and sometimes, {(mainly when she was in middle school); I} was separated from my daughter. Socialization has been null and void. I'm traumatized and so is she. But at least she had school to keep her brain churning. Even my own daughter is not talking to me. Now that she's out of grade school. It's like a worldwide cult against me. The trauma sometimes causes me to say things out loud when I just planned to say them to myself.

Thank God I've been able to write books as I've always wished, as I sit in my daughter's apartment watching my only grandson. If only my knowledge and creativity could be my wealth. But the conspiracy against me that includes my family, not excluding my daughter or father-(at least it seems); is holding me captive to watch my grandson. I'm being threatened that if I get a job, I will be fired; by white people. They are verbally saying this as I sleep. I keep my TV on. The entire world believes that Eric Vaughan was an upright man for me and that I cheated on him. My cousin and her husband in Philly, set me up for murder as well. Understand that this is not paranoia. Everyone believes that when I said "They are obviously saying to themselves, leave her outside until she starts hoing". They believe I'm admitting to selling sex. When in actuality I was being forced by Christians and everyone else, to ride with, and or stay in the home of (strange) men, for shelter! I have no health insurance because they don't want me to have any. I DO NOT SMELL. It was never an issue. I'm verbally harassed now by every race while being forced to ride the bus. They are pretending that I smell. They want me to be the lady from Gone Girl. I have no desire or plan to disappear. Can you believe I'm still considering going to Thanksgiving in Virginia to celebrate with my extended family.

The verbal harassment is so enormous that any job I receive is literally a set-up. Counting money, selling products or teaching a verbally abusive child; all impossible. Yet everyone refuses to buy my books. I know I'm not a ho now nor did I used to be but I'm even being harassed by educated people who believe their smart. I'm being verbally harassed in the House of God.

1. I'm the homeless lady
2. The TV/movie ho; and
3. The single mother who has a college degree, a trade license and no car or house.

Point 5

I have a full rack of clothing that coincide with the clothing worn by actors in countless movies. There are slanderous movies that have been released that date back as far as 35 odd years ago. The movies that I have clothing from are relatively recent. I don't watch the movie and then go buy their outfits. They know what I like and they have clothing situated so that I will choose what's in my size while shopping.

Point 6

I had a few, but now have several anxieties that make getting and keeping employment, challenging. I can't ride in the back of two door coupes. I can't ride on the subway. I can't ride on elevators. I can't ride on an airplane or a charter bus. I can't always breathe when stuck in traffic on an unfamiliar, two-lane back-road that is covered with trees if I don't know where I'm going and/or if we just go to such an unfamiliar road abruptly in the darkness of night. I can't work in a building without windows. And I can't ride through tunnels.

Point 7

If you calculate the cost of the hotel that we stayed in every night, for two to three years, you will have an idea of just how much money I handled during this time. At least until my daughter graduated from high school. It was only enough to pay for the hotel and for food. I received the money on a daily basis. There was a time when we didn't have a kitchen in our hotel so food stamps weren't very helpful. You can't purchase already prepared foods.

Did you calculate the daily cost of a $120 hotel room over 2-3years? It's approximately $40,320 per year. Have you seen the movie FOCUS. No I did not have enough money to hire a civil litigator. I know my daughter and I need to stay focused but I am not a thief. I've never stolen anything in my life. My daughter is not a thief nor is my brother. If I sold sex, I would have kept my apartment and I would have a car.

Point 8

Employers don't seem to want to pay me what I'm worth. I also need to be able to afford healthcare costs, if not healthcare insurance. I suppose it is believed by many that I am slow or 'dumb'. I mention in more than one book that every girlfriend I've ever known is a Surgeon, or Anesthesiologist, a Physicians Assistant, an Attorney, a nurse, an Architect and a Pharmacist. I wasn't saying that I was dumb for not becoming a Scientist. I just never tapped into my fullest potential. I made excellent grades in Advanced Placement classes during school and I love to learn. Although they may be, I was not saying that my girlfriends were wise or kind for becoming what they've become. I needed and still need their friendship, even though I've made a few mistakes in life and did not choose a very tangible career. Who better to socialize wit then peers of 20 years, 30 years and 40 years?

Point 9

Because men are hell-bent on creating ho's in society and woman are hell-bent on creating unproductive citizens.

I noted in one book that my father doesn't hug me nor does my daughter; and that I find myself hugging strangers outside someday's as I pan-handled. Perverts and the whoreminded, assume that I mean strange men can say to me "Can I get a hug" and I'll oblige by rubbing my breast up against them. I meant that "Christian" women would pray for me and then hug me goodbye.

The mind that is hell-bent on seeing things through a perverted eye; reads my Libel and Slander book and understands my explanations of the illusion of (intimate) male company; rather in my dorm room or at my aunt's house, as me falling and being a ho. Instead of the literate eye revealing to them that I've been and I'm still being; sabotaged and lied on.

Further more...

I can't even work as an effective nanny to my grandson. I need to go to the doctors: OB/GYN and internal meds when necessary. I also need to have regular dental visits. If I am unable to use my daughter's phone to get my medical insurance through the state, set -up. I can look for work and assist her in finding a daycare provider but she is desperately trying in conjunction with my father, to make it seem as though I am just leaving her in a lurch. She wats me to just up and leave her like my father left me so that people will believe he did what was right regarding his children when they needed his assistance most; regardless of their ages. (Anyone can lose their job.) The other day, he said my daughter is not going to need me. I suppose he meant once she finishes medical assisting school. I think she truly believes that. She needs Jesus some kind of bad.

Point 10

How can anyone in his or her right mind, expect me to apply
for employment, interview and be successful at such an
attempt when I don't have a dollar to my name? No money to
buy a work uniform. No money to catch the bus. With brain
trauma and brain cell loss. I've been conditioned as if I'm a pet
dog. There's a very large campaign of Lies about how I smell
in public. I have no cell phone. And there's an entire city
intent on making me late for work; to fit the movie scenes.
Honestly. I've always been a morning person. I even found
words in a few of my books that I didn't write, after the final
printing.
Educated people in positions of power are either lacking
kindness, spirituality or wisdom. Those who are not educated
just keep repeating, "It's too late. Everyone believes the lies
about you!"

A forced criminal record in a world where me and my brother
weren't meant to survive because we are obviously being set-
up. Not caring about our well-being, is just like being set-up.

Point 11

Recently, (April 30th, 201), or so; it was discovered that I'm not as claustrophobic as I used to be. The trauma and abuse and harassment hasn't completely made me lose my mind. Leaving me outside hasn't destroyed me. So now, everyone is trying hard to fid a reason to discredit me. I actually applied for work now that I know my daughter's work hours and school schedule. The goal here, is to keep me unemployed. Let me back tract just for a moment. I was working at Wal-Mart and a man who was dressed as a police officer, walked up to me and asked me if I remembered him. As if we'd had a moment or something. I was pan-handling and he had given me a few bucks. But after I left Wal-Mart, I saw him on the news, as a molester. Now, the church where I was asked to fulfill court ordered community service, reveals a news story of a woman who has been sexually abused by the Pastor. Now just coincidentally, I sat in that churches conference room one day as I did my community service, and rubbed my breast, erotically. Just to see if there was a camera. I'm tired of people watching me. No one in the church even mentioned it. But now, that it's convenient to stop me from being hired, there's a major news story that calls for all of the footage at the church. I was only doing community service for pan-handling because I was being forced to pan-handle. I'd written scores of churches in the region and surrounding cities, asking for help. Help with houses for me and my daughter who was still in school, so I wouldn't have to break the law.

I'm Homeless
Please Buy My Poetry Book
By Angela C. Williams
© 2004/© 2015

I know it's sad that I've memorized a poem by Langston Hughes, (I Dream a World), ever since middle school but have yet to memorize one of my own poems. That is my goal for this upcoming summer.

Would you like to read some of my poems? :

Hang In There

I used to think it was the smiles of strangers passing by,
I thought it was the precious songs from birds up in the sky;
I used to think it was the laughter from the joke I heard,
I thought it was the joy I felt from others I had served;
I used to think it was the cash I saved I my account,
I thought it was the old wise word I heard up on the mount;
I used to think the sunny days were special just because,
I think I know the reason now and boy how wrong I was;
It's the rain that makes the sunny days so special and so great,
Cause when it rains, for sunny days, my friend, I just can't wait;
Sunny days are coming, yes, hang in there, don't cry,
For I am always with you, I am your Indigo Skye.

Indigo Skye is my daughter's name. 'May be cute but I'm just a substitute, but deep inside I'm blue.' That's pretty funny.

(The Christmas card given to each extended family member for Christmas 2001)

May you delight in the splendor of colors
That cross your face this season.

May your eyes be glad.
May you embrace the harmony of sounds
That fall upon your ears.
May you get lost in your imagination
As you experience the softness of the fabrics
That flow across your finger tips.
May the aroma that fills your home,
Lure you closer to the heartbeat of every family gathering;
Thank God for great food.
May the hope that fills your spirit,
Penetrate your every thought to bring peace, serenity,
And joy into the core of your life.
May you stay in good health, prosper,
And be a blessing to others.
But most of all, may every breath that you take
Remind you of the reason that we celebrate Christmas.
Christ was born to die for us.
He loves us and we should love one-another.

No Title

When life takes a crazy turn and things seem so 'a rye',
When family that you've known for years begin to pass you
by,
When friends and those who were around, look dazed and
cold and hard;
When everything that comes about, it leaves your heart so
scarred.

What do you do when the only ones who open up their arms,
Are those whom you don't know their names but grace you
with their charms.
It's twisted and it's strangely odd to think that it's that way,
To embrace the hugs of passers-by but hugs from friends are
stray.

Some Poems from Middle School and High School

Where Are You?

I see you from the outside, Although it is not you
For you are only spirit, for God has made you true.
To live for him is to live right and share your natural beauty,
To fake your hair and then your face, you must feel it a duty.

He gave you hair and then a face, without some could not live,
No everybody does not receive, they accent the positive.

In search of style ad glamour too, it may be in a store.
Yet morals for the inside, are always real décor.

If you're the face behind the case and case is left abroad;
Are you not there, I see your face, or is it just a fraud?

Although you say he's ugly, she's pretty by and by.
We've never seen each other once it's all a great big lie.

We often make decisions from appearance and/or skin.
And some go even further, the favor sides of men.

So ask yourself, where am I and answer with a grin,
The joy and happiness I feel, it all comes from within.

(Because we always went to separate schools)

Felita My Friend

We grew together as one my dear, our friendship of course
will always be here.
I miss not seeing you every day- I guess that God just planned
it that way.
Sometimes we walk alone you see- that's just the way it has to
be.
I love you still of course you know-just keep in touch and
we'll still grow.
I wrote this poem in hopes to say;
Have a Very Happy Valentine's Day

To Little Nicky

To my Nicole, I'm glad you're here; you make me smile from
year to year.
We've been together for so very long; it's so plain to see our
relationship is strong.
We're friends; and friends are hard to find-we treat each other
oh so kind.
We laugh, we love, we smile, we share- in time of need for
each other we're there.

Our friendship sure has come along way,
Have a Very Happy Valentine's Day

My Dearest Randy

I write this poem for you my dear because I love you so.
I need you in my life sweetheart, I just want you to know.

Without you I feel emptiness inside my weakened soul-
And every night I dream of you; Its you I need to hold.

I often think; what brought us here and what might take us
out.
All I know, is we belong; and that, there is no doubt.

Once in our lives we strayed away and we could hardly live-
But soon God brought another day and something had to
give.
Cause love is something shared between two people who
really care.
Even when the time may come that I cannot be there.
You'll know my heart is with you just recall those summer
days.
And think of how we expressed our love in very touching
ways.

It's Valentine's Day Sweetheart you know,
And I'm often given candy.
But it's not every day I receive a gift-
As sweet as my dearest Randy.

(I was mad at my parents and I packed a small suitcase and
ran away to the front porch for the day.)

Too Young to Know

You argues with your parents then decided you were grown.
I do not need their money I can make it on my own.
I'll leave and then I'll find a job and somewhere nice to stay.
They'll see that I've decided, to walk my own set way.
I'm ready to get by in life by making my decisions.
Who cares if temporarily, I'm sleeping with the pigeons.
It may be fun, you never know just who you may run into.

I'm sure there's someone out there with money they will lend you.
They'll see that I am tired and hungry by and by.
They'll say to their dear parents, Oh please don't let her die".
I'll put a great act on for them; they can't help but feel pity.
But then again it may not work; I am in New York City.
I do remember back at home, I walked down one dark street.
I walked real fast and shook my head, not one head did I greet.
But wait who is this coming, I see him with a gun.
For some strange reason now it seems street-life is not that fun.
I think that I will call my mom and ask for my return.
I'll let her know that this here day, my lesson I have learned.
They're crazy people out here, and no they do not care.
I'd rather be at home right now, although you're still unfair.

(I was not really alone in New York City)

No Title

When summer turns to rain; the forgotten season.
The water continues to fall, with no place to go.
It has a personality of it's own, it falls to earth
        to make friends with the fish and the dolphins
          but it still doesn't have a face.
It only takes on the face of those who stare at it.
It catches the tears of those who look down upon it.
It washes the feet of those who step on it.
It quenches the thirst of every mouth
        that makes itself available to drink.
It is everywhere.
It is us.

(When School Leaves a Lasting Impression)

Farewell

I came to you four years ago, not knowing what to do,
> But you accepted me my friend; so far you have been
true.
The first year was the greatest, I had myself a ball;
> The second year was different, my grades began to fall.

I gained some friends but lost a few, it hurt me to my heart.
> I think again, oh we're still friends; we just have grown
apart.

It's something when you take a look; they're freshman coming
in;
> You realize that you were there; you see where you
have been.
To some it may not be as deep as I have made it seem,
> But you come without a care, I say, and leave out with
a dream.

To finish school and be your best it's what you're shooting for,
> You take one small step at a time to find that open
door.

Through trying times we cried and cried and suffered good
and plenty.
> But later on to college halls, my teachers, they had sent
me.
They sent me to the hardest school but much I have to show.
> Good-bye sweet friends and Largo High; I'll really miss
you so.

Largo Pride

When I think of all the fun we've had, it's hard to say good-
bye.
The memories, when thought about, seem to make me cry.
The times we've spent together, sometimes they turned out
sad.
But patiently we made it through. The goods out-weighed the
bad.
The tears, the smiles, the thoughts we've shared, have brought
us to this day.
It's wonderful to see that you have not been led astray.
The anxiousness and eagerness I know it's in your heart.
But as we walk, each step we take, will lead us farther apart.
So as you leave with happiness and joy down deep inside.
Good luck in all your endeavors; and don't forget that Largo
Pride.

Poetry Written After High School

Carlos

I know you're keeping busy, as time just passes by.
You're happy and your silly, you're such a friendly guy.
I'm glad you've met a lady friend, who knows how great you
are.
I don't have much money to lend, even though we're famous
stars.

They immortalized us on the screen and told our storied
wrong.
I hope to drive up on the scene, and hope it won't take long.

I hope you're staying fit these days, I miss the fun we've shared.
I hope you come back with us and know I've always cared.

Imagine If Everything was Clear

With open eyes, we see things that help is learn,
With open hands, we feel things that sting and burn,
With open ears, we hear sounds that chirp and chew,
With open mouths, we speak love is so true,

With open minds, we think of better ways,
With open arms, we gladly give our praise,
With open doors, we spread a lot of cheer,
With open hearts, the world is seen as clear.

And when you see things clearly, you are a better you.
You can be more productive; cause better is your view.
So if you can't tell where to go by sitting I the chair.
Try standing on the table, you'll see better from the air.
It may look strange to passers-by but you don't know their hue.
They may see everything as dull and you want to see it true.
So climb on up and look around, you'll see things from the top.
You'll feel sense of urgency to strive, and never stop.

Be the best you, you can be!

Trials of a Relationship

Life has taken both of us through stress and grief and pain,
And even to this day it seems, the sadness yet remains.
We struggle and we work each day, survival never stops,
And when we ponder purpose, our momentum level drops.

So let us not ask questions of how and when and why,
Let's trust that all is well because on we He has His eye.
If I could change the world events, I wouldn't change a thing,
I've learned that what can't kill me, a stronger day it brings.

I had a box of chocolates on my job the other day,
It seemed to symbolize my life in every single way.
From outside it was candy, I knew it would be sweet,
From inside, I just didn't know, which one that I should eat.

But either try to go away, I knew it would be sweet,
And sadly on first taste it said, I'm sorry but you lose.
But when I tried another one, how happy I became,
The inside tasted better, the outside looked the same.

It's scary though to think that life is simplified to such,
But if we think about it, it actually means quite much.
So when your days are long and hard remember what I say,
There's someone who would love to stand, or see, or kneel
and pray.

So every chance you get my friend, just praise His Holy name,
And every chance I get my love, I'll gladly do the same.
On two things I can rest assured when my life has come to end
I will be with my Jesus and I'll know that you're my friend.

Thought for the month: January 1992
Love…a feeling; an expression, an atmosphere.
What do the words "I-love-you" have to do with love in
actuality?
Not much.
One could love a person and it be known without them ever
saying a word.
So where do they connect?
Just as its written, love is in between the lines…I-love-you.
In between the words pronounced, in between the flowers
bought, I between the love that is made…
I-love-you..Three simple words used to brighten someone's
day.
Love- a way to live your life.

Write A Letter

The distance, oh it's hard enough, I'm east and you are west.
I asked you for one letter, you said you'd try your best.
Your best is far from true I see, because my mail is none.
I know you have a busy life, I know you have much fun.

But do you think of me my love, when you are way out there.
I haven't seen a mere postcard, my love do you still care.

I don't ask much, you do not call, for cost I understand.
But letter, postcard, telegraph, my love I must demand.

I pray for you, you pray for me, through God our love is strong.
But no contact for weeks and months, for me that's just too long.

Insight

In love, we find romances.
In life, we take our chances.
In peace, we find our strength.
In hope, our thoughts are spent.

In fear, we won't sleep well.
In doubt, we mustn't dwell.
Instead, we've got to know.
In god, our faith will grow.

(I must have been imagining someone writing a poem to me)

You are the most beautiful flower that I have ever seen.
You are such a sweet fragrance.
You are a sight for sore eyes.
You are so giving. So caring. And so unselfish.
You are a queen. A precious gem.
You ae the love that sustains my soul.
You saw past my faults when I was less than perfect.
You forgave me and continued to love.
You ae every breath that I take.
You are my eternal love.

Choose Him

He's needed and not wanted, oh yes how He is sad-
You constantly defy Him and yes He too gets mad.
But now He has decided for those who don't receive,
His creation will destroy you, and this you must believe.
You can go on forever, oh please don't get me wrong,
For those of us who live in truth, our lives will be so long.
Maybe not on earth we'll stay, we may die of no cause,
Just think He just might want you there because He saw no
flaws.
Just take a chance, you'll never know if you decide to wait.
You might wake-up; yes I said might; it just may be too late.

To Die for

Now what do you mean saying you don't want to die,
There's a land full of treasures that waits I the sky.
More peace and contentment that we could have dreamed,
And It's just where we're going if we are redeemed.

It's scary to think that we won't breathe again,
And to fathom the thought of us leaving our friends.
But however you twist it we all have to go,
So who will be first, I guess we'll never know.

The way of our passing is what we all dread,
Cause tragedies can't seem to clear from our head.
Today they seem vast, prolonged and extreme,
And we can't figure out, just what it all means.

Diseases are rampant; there's famine and war,
There's child abuse, murder and thieves at our door.

From plane bombs to car crashes we don't decide,
For God only knows, when we'll take our last ride.

But for now, let's know, that all things; they work for our good,
Of those who do love Him and do what they should.
So death let's not fear it, let's fear God and live,
And for His forgiveness, our lives we must give.

Galatians 5:22

What is a card that's never sent;
What is a dime that is never spent;
What is a tear that never falls;
What is a house that has no walls.
What is a tree without its root;
What is a Christian without God's fruit.
      A missing link in a war so real;
      A hollow center which Satan could fill.
So let us be mindful, and let us take heed.
Walk in love at all times. It's first in our creed.

Our Love

When all our hopes and dreams were closed, you quickly found the key-
I know loves not worth money, but priceless o would be.
You took your very soul my love and touched my broken heart-
My world was very incomplete, when we were far apart.
I feel you in your absence, so deep is all my love-
Because it comes from Jesus Christ; from heaven up above.

A Woman In Waiting

To feel you with my spirit, not with my finger tips

To taste you with my thoughts and not my luscious lips
To speak a little comfort-to you without a word
To know that looking in my eye each passage you have heard
To hold you deep within my heart, not even with my arms
To know the meaning of your smile and love your winning charm
To open up my soul to you, to let you in my life
To tell you yes when I am asked if I will be your wife.

Today

I close my eyes and darkness falls but I can see your face,
Your beauties like a flame to me, you light a tarnished place.
My heart was down, I missed the love that used to live within,
In you I'm filled with peace and joy each moment that I spend.
You lift me up when broken dreams tear deep into my soul,
Some reason I feel strongly that our love will not grow cold.
I wrote these words to let you know, in a special way;
I wish you happy days to come, especially today.

Together At Last

Happiness I seem to find in every drop of rain,
I'd rather not the sun to shine because it brings me pain;
When he is gone so far from me a ear comes to my eye,
The rain it helps my grief to fade because it hides my cry;
The sun reminds me of the fun that we just cannot share,
But if I had the chance my friend you know you'd find me there;
I long to walk the narrow aisle with you holding my hand,
Strengthened love as one we'd find in this here pagan land;
We'd lead the lost straight to his knees to find their joy within,
That they might see the love he has and how their hearts He'd mend;
Until that day I'll pray and pray, our souls He'll bond as one,
And I'll live right and give my all because He gave His Son.

Abstract

It's a thing, it's a noun.
It's an action, it's a verb.
It's a choice.
It's a command.
It's an intangible feeling.
It's an unrehearsed behavior.
It's a long period of time.
It's every moment.

What or Who are you?

I'm an undefined expression waiting happen
In every situation you encounter.

Joy & Pain

I've seen a lot to be only 28.
I've searched my life; time didn't wait.
The days of yester have come & gone.
I've sat, I've cried from dusk 'til dawn.

I cannot figure out the why.
Some days I'm low, some days I'm high.
A little bit of both is best.
A mixture makes a joyful guest.

The sun &rain they must be one.
Without each other, their days are done.
They must respect each other as they pass.
Cause if they meet a storm is cast.

What Am I?

I am the essence of it all.
Without me there is nothing.
I am how life is formed.
If you drop me a lot I am very powerful.
It is always difficult to contain me.
I fall from above.
I run down below.
I float through the air.
I rise into space.
I twirl and cause doom.
I make up over 80% of the earth and 80% of the human body.
I give life to any and everything that lives.

No Title

When happy is watching your favorite sports team win a
game-
When happy is choosing the chocolate that is filled with
caramel-
When happy is hearing your favorite song on the radio-
When happy is finding the perfect shoes to match your dress-
When happy is knowing that you made the day of a stranger.

Think Lovingly

It's amazing how love transcends everything and anything we
could ever imagine-
Hope endures through every disappointment & devastation-
Will-to, can drive the smallest thought through obstacles
That led to everlasting contentment and fulfillment.

No Title

Thank you daddy for your loving correction when I'm wrong.
Thank you for taking time to show me how to do new things.
Thank you for encouraging me to always domy best.
Thank for being you!
Happy Father's Day
A father's love helps to make us who we are.
Your hard work has never gone unnoticed.
This card is just a small token of my appreciation to you
for all that you have done, and continue to do,
to make life pleasant for me and so many others.

Happy Father's Day

Together We Stand
What's the matter with our people,
Don't criticize let's build.
That's the problem with our children,
Don't throw stones, let's be their shield.
What's the situation in our cities,
Please, let's stop the crime.
Start a business, create jobs,
Since you cannot spare a dime.
Volunteer to help each other,
Let your time here leave a mark.
Let's not leave our precious youth,
Hopelessly wandering in the dark.
Take their hand, guide their journey,
Tell them not to fight the fight,
Show them how to win the battle.
Lead them to the shinning light.
You artists have the power.

You're inspiring by and by.
Write the movies, sing the songs
That will spark a natural high.
They hear the muck and mire ,
repeated in the verse.
They see the video you made
for sex and money, now they thirst.
Well, let's feed them healthy knowledge,
Through entertainment, school and home.
The world can be a scary place,
If we face it all alone.

Divided We Fall

This is an excerpt from my book: Libel and Slander Of Angela Williams-

My School-Aged Years

I haven't always been homeless. In fact I lived a great childhood and my early adult life started out plush and very eventful. One might say I felt very lucky; blessed even.
It was a neighborhood with two entrances. Neither had a sign that let a driver know that they had arrived. You were now in Ritchie Manor off of Ritchie Road; where the children went to Ritchie Elementary and in my home, they lived on Richville Drive and watched the cartoon, Richie Rich. Our house was small but it had 4 bedrooms and 1 ½ bathrooms. No dishwasher, no fireplace and no pantry. I can only speak for our household when I say. We weren't rich, but we didn't want for anything. Oh, and did I tell you that Woody Wood Pecker lived behind my house? ("No"). Well, he did.

Our neighborhood was full of young kids who enjoyed playing together. My house was in the back of the neighborhood on the last street. Our house was in the middle of our street. There was no house directly across from us so when we hosted our large family for cook-outs, there was always somewhere to park. The location of our home was great for kick-ball and dodge ball. The sidewalk was perfect for double-dutch and roller skating. There was only one thing we had to worry about. The neighborhood terror. This new family moved in two doors down and brought this frightening German Shepard. You would think that they would have purchased a thicker chain or a taller fence. For ten years, he popped his chain and chased the nearest person into a frenzy. He actually bit a few people. You wanna know his name? He has the same name as the toy doll who comes to life and stabs his victims to death. He has the same name as the big mouse with the pizza adventure land for, children's birthdays.

We had a dog for a little while when I was 5. He used to pop his chain too but he didn't bite people. Eventually, he ran away. I guess looking back, they were both scared of the animals in the woods behind our homes.

My mother always had birthday parties for me and my brother. It's warm during my birthday and it falls near a holiday and sometimes Spring Break. We would usually not have trouble getting the entire family to come to a cook-out during a holiday; and even our numerous family friends.

My mother used to manage a bank and believe it or not she used to take me to work with her when I was really little; I remember. She was good friends with a lady from India. She shared the name of the puppy on the cartoon Arthur. It was really fun. She eventually left to work for the postal service, like my father. He's worked the night shift ever since I could remember. My mother worked her way up to supervisor but he chose to keep his position and shift. I'm saddened when I think that neither me nor my brother were in a position to take care of our parents the way they took care of us. But at least they had each other after we left.

Although my mom was not a haunted Plymouth vehicle, she drove very fast. That is her name. Christine, like the movie. She called her bosses, Boss and she was married to a mouse whom she could never catch, in a silent cartoon. Yes that's my dad's name. Well it's just like the ocean…under the moon…; no my brother is not a Spanish singer but he shares his first name. (Give us your heart, make it real or just forget about it).

Our parents worked hard but they played hard too. They loved to travel. When we were young, they took us everywhere. We had a conversion van that allowed us to take road trips in comfort, before gas prices were high and unstable. When we were very young, we flew once and drove down a few years later, to Sea World and Disney World in Orlando, Florida. After my mother's brother was relocated to Wisconsin by his employer, we drove way up there to visit. When I was ten and my brother was sixteen, we drove in a caravan with two other families from the neighborhood, to the World's Fair in New Orleans, Louisiana. Our male cousin who share the name of the son on *The Fresh Prince*, went with us. Everybody had a riding partner. My father or brother rode with me. I forgot to tell you why I couldn't get in the pool at the hotel. A week or so before our trip, I was riding my ten speed with the girl who invited me to play basketball, on the back of my bike. We got up our speed so that when we passed the house with the big dog, we would just sail on by. I didn't work out that way. He was in the front and his bark scared me so much that I crashed my bike. She walked home and I walked my bike home. Bloody and scarred, (obviously discombobulated), I tucked myself into bed. My brother was in his room and my dad was downstairs watching TV. When my mom got home she came in my room and I was bloody and scarred. She yelled at both of them. I couldn't remember where we fell; she asked me. We had to go get my friend and she told my mom what happened. (I didn't have restrictions as to where I could ride within the neighborhood. I wasn't lying. I truly didn't remember). I'm not a doctor so I didn't know that I needed x-rays and a scan of my brain. I had stitches and a big giant bandage on my side. My mom keep it clean and changed my bandage regularly but my trip was not quite as fun as it probably could have been. But it's OK because my brother and I had a lot of stuff around the house to keep us busy. We played cars, Battleship, Connect Four and even had out own arcade sized pinball machine. Every Friday our parents bought dinner from a different carry-out and sometimes we would play Bingo.

Speaking of stiches; my former friend, the surgeon; sister of the anesthesiologist, used to play dolls and house with me and the girls in my neighborhood. Me, her and another little girl, were lying on the ground pretending to be in bed and I needed more space, so I told her to roll-over. She fell down from ground level to the bottom of the basement steps, right in front of the basement door. She busted her chin. We had to rush her to the emergency room. You would think that experience led her to become a doctor but not quite.

Two of my mother's female friend's had a devastating health issue at a much younger age. Fortunately, they survived. The mother of these two previously mentioned doctors, had an aneurism. The mother of the young woman whose first name is my middle name; had breast cancer. They are both still alive and well.

A few years later, for a couple of weeks during the summer, my mom and dad sent me and my brother (alone on a plane) to visit her other brother and his family in Melbourne, Florida. Although he lived in Greece many years before he was stationed in Melbourne, we didn't fly overseas as a family to visit.

I ended up going to Europe in the 9ᵗʰgrade with the French Club. I was taking Spanish, but it was an opportunity that I didn't want to miss. I celebrated my 15ᵗʰ birthday in Europe. It was great. I've never been attacked by a bidet-(*BAPS*). I've never fallen in love with one either- (*Jumping the Broom*). I'd never seen one and I used it once when we first got there. My super fantastic moment of celebration can actually be matched by a super scary moment when I left my purse on the train; in (I believe it was), Switzerland. As I exited the train, I realized my purse was not with me. It had my traveler's checks inside. I don't remember if our chaperone held on to all of our passports or not, but I ran back down the platform and onto the train. I was frantic hoping that the train didn't pull off. I grabbed my purse and rejoined my group. In hind-sight I guess being separated from my group and lost in another country would have been much worse than replacing my traveler's checks.

Both sides of my family has always had family reunions on a fairly regular basis. My father's side more frequently than my mom. I don't know which is true. My mother's side of the family stopped having reunions after my mom passed away or after my younger female cousins got married. I think they are all keeping their men locked away for safe keeping.

My father's, mother's, brother's, wife (or his aunt, through marriage) is still living and we are still in touch with that extended family. Meet them. May I introduce them? I only eat the Brown M&M's cause chocolates already Brown. They are very nice and they are all very accomplished. (Mind you; that is the last name of the young lady whose birthday is on September 11ᵗʰ; and my grandmother's maiden name). Our reunion is always the weekend of my grandmother's birthday. I guess I'll see them this fall. Here's the catch. My only nephew graduates from high school this spring near Tampa. If I ride down there with my dad and stay so that I can move to Miami near my brother I won't make it to my grandson's first family reunion. Who will watch my grandson?

When I was in elementary school, my father's dad was found dead on the sidewalk out-side of his home. He had apparently fallen or been thrown from his high-rise apartment window. I've never read the police report, however I wouldn't be surprised to find conflicting evidence. Could the movies, Beverly Hills Cop and I Robot be eluding to the need for a new investigation.

If you are a parent; whether you're obese or not, and you over heard your fifth grader on the phone talking about her boyfriend, would you be devastated. If you had a fifth grader who ate twice as much food during each meal, as your other children; would you be concerned. What if he or she didn't eat vegetables? What about smoking cigarettes or drinking alcohol? Are either of these reasons to stop either child from participating in extracurricular activities? You may not stop them but you definitely need to encourage them. Please keep in mind as you read; I do not have any addictions, nor have I ever. I've never smoked anything or abused alcohol or drugs. I was invited to go to basketball practice with a friend of mine from the neighborhood when I was 9 years old. (A friend who shares the same last name as the scary family who named their daughter Wednesday). From that day forward I was hooked on the game. (Or maybe I was hooked on all the new friends and fun I was now having). Every season I played a sport with the community Boys and Girls Club. When football time rolled around; I cheered. I played basketball in the winter and softball in the summer. A lot of times, my mother, carpooled a lot of us to practice. We were really good. We had two coaches and one of them was, my (former) best friend and team-mates; father. Our other coach was an older white man who owned a property in Ocean City. Every summer he took three of us to the beach for a weekend. Including our other coach's daughter of course. Life was fun. I only wished I had encouraged my brother to get involved in Boys and Girls Club activities. I wonder why no young men invited him. I wonder what prompted her to invite me.

My mom took us to see Ice Capades every time they came into town.

My mother was like the team mom. She even got an award for being so dedicated to our team; during boys and girls club and high school. My dad worked at night so he missed all of my High school basketball games. The year I ran track; he traveled with us everywhere.

My mom loved to shop. I remember keeping a calendar on my wall logging every outfit; being sure not to wear anything twice in one month during high school. Even when I was smaller I was particular about my outfits. I recall walking through a department store with my mom wearing my all purple outfit to match my newly painted bedroom. (I asked if they could paint my room purple). I was walking with her and she said, "Where is your other shoe?" I said, "It's back there stuck in the escalator." My new purple Jordache sneaker. We went back to get it. I believe I was in the fourth grade.

I remember in elementary school when my mother bought her first dream car. She and my brother picked me up from 6th grade, in a really nice, brand-new, BMW. Unfortunately, my dad totaled it. (Not before my former friend, the Anesthesiologist, used it for her high school prom. But the important thing is that he is OK. His rib broke and punctured his lung. (The actor/actress is driving my mother's car in the movie Machete).

I remember my mother dropping me and my life-long neighbor and friend, (the spice from Gilligan's Island), at bible study on some Sundays. She and I played Barbie dream house in our basements on numerous occasions. We got our first ten-speed bikes on the same Christmas.

The dark side of my basement will always be like the dark side of the moon to me. (…..nothing to do with Mulan). I could never reach my arm around and turn on the light for fear that the monster would get my arm. So I would always fall to sleep on the couch and my brother would come downstairs, pick me up, put me in the bed and tuck me in.

I was taking a lot of dance classes at a small Fashion Institute that was preparing me to compete in the MISS TEEN Pageant; where I won 1st runner up; I was 14. Having the support of an entire community of friends, family and my parents' co-workers, was an awesome feeling. It almost felt surreal, being on stage with that many people clapping for you. (Angelica from the movie; *Six Days, Seven Nights;* my talent: my dance and my out-fit). Well, my hips aren't narrow anymore and my breast may actually be big enough now, too bad I don't look like her. Maybe I could have snagged my green-eyed friend from Wild World Amusement Park.

Oh yeah. That was my first job ever. I met a lot of people. Including my first love. I saw him and wanted to meet him. I was introduced and as I glanced at the other guys in the landscaping department, I immediately became overtaken by another guy. This green-eyed hunk. But it was too late. I composed myself and began a great love affair with the guy who was just as excited to meet me. Guess what happened. My new boyfriend, offered me a ride home. Great! Not great. The gorgeous hunk, was his best friend. He was riding home with us. No I didn't cheat. He was an OK boyfriend. Our mothers talked to one-another and everything. During the summer, he took me to the movies and a few times we returned to work on our day off, to enjoy the fun of the amusement park. Our mother's visited with each other and everything.

He even came to my first dance in high school. I don't remember him inviting me to any of his dances. Our relationship was strained because he didn't attend the same school as I did. Everyone was telling me that he had cheated on me with a girl at his school. They told me her name and everything. I think he must have been just flirting with her. (Oh, a plan to break us up-*High School Musical*). When I wasn't in school I was busy with sports. He was busy in the spring with baseball. They both played for their school. Something in my heart felt different. (Maybe he was mad because he was really overdressed at the Back-To-School Dance). I didn't know he was going to be all dressed up. He never invited me to go out anymore. After a year or so he and I broke up but we were still friends. I had a few other boyfriends during high school. Those relationships didn't last very long. I'm not sure what was said. We talked for a while once and I'm sure we entertained getting back together. But me and my first love ended up 'breaking up for good', (on the phone), right before the prom. I didn't cheat on him or anyone else. (Might not make sense to you, but it's the world of teen-agers). I decided that we shouldn't go to the prom together. I ended up going alone.

{He led the Redskins to victory in Super Bowl 22. (Just say his name over and over out loud to yourself). I had not long before, had sex for the first time in my life, with my boyfriend-(my first love). But my father sure watches a lot of sports on TV. He could probably draw out some plays. He even looks a little like him}. OMG. So this is the other reason why my high school coach gave me his daughter's jersey number; 22?

For the next year or so, I became closer friends with my ex's best friend. We talked on the phone. It was a while before I actually went over to his home. I think it all started when I found myself talking to him about being mad at my boyfriend years ago when he made me mad.

On prom night, I went to dinner at a restaurant on the water, with a group of friends, (other couples); before the Prom. Guess who I danced with during the first slow song? My Physics teacher. I thought I looked great and I felt beautiful. It was a great night. I went to a Prom after party at a hotel. It wasn't really my scene so I didn't stay long. Then I went to my green-eyed friend's house so he could see how pretty I looked. We slept on the basement floor in front of the TV; fully clothed, all nite; he snuck me in. No we didn't touch. The next morning I went home changed my clothes and went to Kings Dominion with the same group of friends of which I'd gone to the pre-Prom dinner.

Well, he moved to Florida and opened a Fitness Gym. Did I mention that the one and only time he came to my house, when high school was ending; he brought me a roll of cookie dough. He walked in, handed it to me and walked right back out? Yes I knew and still know how to make cookies in the oven, the proper way; I don't need Ingrid from Uptown Girls, to show me. *Clueless*. They're both married; and have been for some time now. Well, anyway....Maybe I'll see him and his family when I go visit my brother. Maybe I won't. Maybe I'll run into my ex when I'm 50, and he'll be single; I doubt it because the last time I ran into him, he was really rude. I'm not sure why. When I ran into him while pan-handling a few years back he came to my hotel and played scrabble with me. Back to b-ball with my girls:

When it was time for high school, many of us were used to playing ball together so we won a lot of games even though we were short. We made it to the State Championship all four years. We made it; but we came in second every time. (Our coach always said "No one ever remembers who comes in second"). *Welcome Home Roscoe Jenkins.* I don't know what they feed those Broadneck girls; they were all ginormous!

I recall my girlfriend's, sister's boyfriend moving to Colorado. She shares the name of the daughter of the 42nd President. He was in the Air Force and that was where he was stationed. She decided to attend college out there to be near him. Me and my girlfriend flew out to visit her sister during our spring-break. Colorado is absolutely breath-taking. And although her relationship didn't work out and she had a baby before she finished college, she completed medical school on the East-Coast and is now an Anesthesiologist. You go girl!

My mother's friend worked for an entertainment company and was able to get her tickets to some major concerts. During the last two years of high school, during college and a few years after college; me and my mom, were blessed enough to get great seats to the concerts of, Janet Jackson, Michael Jackson and Maxwell. My mother and I went to see Michael but I was able to invite a friend to go with me to see the other artists.

Even though I didn't accept the basketball scholarship to Salisbury, I played intramural basketball at Towson, for fun and exercise. Ok, I should have known to join a media club of some sort even if I wasn't guided to do so. I guess I hadn't really decided what part of Mass Comm I'd desired to work. I remember speaking with my green-eyed friend who was attending Hampton. He shared with me that he would be transferring to another college because his current school did not have his particular major.

I decided to join a Christian Sorority called ANQ. I recall driving down to Atlanta, Georgia to a Christian Conference with 3 of my frat brothers and 3 of my sorors. There was a snow storm brewing, but we'd already paid our money so we took our time and took turns driving the minivan we'd rented. I was friends with a lot of male and female freshmen on campus. But the new, third-string, freshman quarterback introduced me to my husband. He said we sounded a lot alike when it came to the things of God. No I did not allow him to spend the night. We spent the majority of our time hanging out in my apartment and working out on the track. My soon to be husband, was too busy anyway. He was in and out of town and focused on trying to become a pro-ball player. He was a cornerback. He left school, before graduating to play on the Redskins practice squad. He only had 11 credits to go but that was a chance of a life-time. His jersey number was 22. My jersey number was 22.

During this period, my parents were traveling a lot. Long cruises to the cost of Mexico and other Islands; a trip to Alaska, a trip to Africa. And a train ride across country. Thanks *Home Alone* for the credits that may have led my mom to travel. Who knew she would get sick at such a young age.

Now during my relationship with my soon to be husband, I was very focused on graduating. He was traveling and trying to land a contract with the Redskins. I was wondering why I hadn't been invited to meet his mom and dad yet. Come to find out, his ex-girlfriend had fought with her mom and was staying at his mother's. (He lived there too). His parents didn't know for a long time that there was someone else. He called me from LA one night talking 'bout SHE was with him and she said she was pregnant. I cried for months. He had taken her to the Redskins cook-out while he was supposed to be with me. By the way, you know that girl who sucked the former president's penis; yeah, that was his ex-girlfriends name. (Is that what he wanted from me?) Come to find out, she wasn't pregnant and she left him when he got cut from the Redskins practice squad. He showed up a year later at my door, with flowers; in tears. Against my friends and family member's advice, I took him back. He didn't even have a job. I graduated and found a job as a Reprographics Assistant in the Graphics Department of an Architect firm. I told him that if we were going to continue having sex and he wanted to spend the night, we had to get married. But we planned our wedding. Three months later I was pregnant. I named my daughter after the character in *Mo' Better Blues*. (I was not pregnant when I got married). No, the movie wasn't about me and I've never been to Harlem, but I was dark skinned, and I'd won. It's so sad that things happened the way they did. I, (we), gave up on our marriage so soon. (I wish we'd traveled to an island or taken a cruise for our honeymoon). We went to the Poconos. Can you blame me for trying to form a solid marriage union at an early age?

The new Cinderella movie just came out last week. The light-skinned actor from Mo' Better Blues, shares my last name; in real-life. So I guess she is the real Cinderella. Cause I'm still single. Lol. Maybe I'm still single because an actor/actress whose name in real–life happens to be the same as mine, said in a movie called Waiting to Exhale; when asked about her failed marriage by a fellow actor, that she was not about to go out and find herself a new owner.

Speaking of failed marriage; I suppose the theme song, "Are you that special someone?", from Dr. Doolittle (1998) and the name Blossoms Mammoth Circus; has nothing to do with me being hurt by men who didn't take a relationship with me, seriously (After my divorce). I just noticed the Mammoth Circus scene at the end of the movie, today. May, 2015.

Back on campus:

It seemed as if those who didn't come to school with their best friends, became best friends with their room-mates. My room-mate was from my high-school but, unfortunately she didn't make the grades and lost her scholarship. She was smart but she became a sweetheart to a frat boy and the rest is history. She ended up leaving. She ended up at a larger University and has since graduated and is doing fine. My closest girlfriends had gone to school at Hampton and at MD Eastern Shore where there were a lot of guys from our area and our high school. I wonder if any of my friends ever fell sexually with any of them. I'm kind of surprised that it took them so long to find a life-mate and to have children.

I ended up with a nice White room-mate when I moved off campus. One of my sorors introduced us. She was barely home because she took a job as a nanny for a couple of young children in a neighboring county. I think I sort of pushed her away when I tried to minister to her one day. When she was home, her boyfriend from Bethany Beach was there too. A very attractive black guy. He spent the night quite often. That is not why I ministered to her though.

I remember my parents driving up to my gospel choir concert. It was really nice. My mom also drove up for my induction into the sorority. My pharmacist friend and her mom drove up for the induction as well.

My brother had sort of been coerced into enlisting in the military, right out of high school. He joined the Marines. I know he doesn't regret it. I remember going to his Graduation Ceremony in Parris Island, South Carolina. Soon after, he was stationed in Yuma, Arizona. He told me it was so hot there that you could see the heat rising from the ground. He might as well had been stationed in Africa!.... Well, not quite. You can't take a cross-country road trip home, from Africa. Can you believe he caught the bus home! (One day I hope to drive my daughter cross country to see the west coast). (According to her, she doesn't fly). He'd decided to get out of the military. He married shortly before me but we had our child shortly before them. Long story short, neither marriage worked out. I was home, he was home, and my entire family came from miles around; crossed states even; to celebrate my daughters first birthday (It was my mother's sister's birthday too). My brother was the clown at her party. That was the theme. It was a cook-out. My daughter's father was there too. Unfortunately my husband didn't take the opportunity that posed itself, to try to rekindle our flame, other than attempting to sleep in the same bed with me. It was clearly over. Can you believe his mother called me talking bout' "he has needs". Not, He loves you and we should try to work it out by going on vacation; but, "he has needs". No, I did not have sex with him.

Now if you think that all of the situations with womanizers in college and the negative outcome with my marriage should make me aware of how volatile relationships with guys can be, you have to wonder why I only am able to have male friends after I return home from a failed marriage. A group of girlfriends rallying around me and helping me thrive again would have been very appropriate. Can't say I didn't try to make that happen.

Apparently, my brother couldn't find a permanent place to live (until he could get back on his feet). Not one family member. I don't remember saying he couldn't live with me and I had literally just gotten keys to my apartment. He and his wife had a son the same age as my daughter and they had recently broken up as well.

I know my brother's heart must have been broken and I feel bad. When a black male has one or two negative things happen in the early part of his life; he can definitely begin life with a defeated attitude.{ Especially if two of those things are as important as finding shelter or a minor record due to something simple like traffic violations, or finance (bad credit). I'm just saying; in general, with black men....}

He left for Miami. He never moved back to this area. The tears of a clown-when no one's around. I might be cute but I ended up just being a substitute; deep inside I'm blue? Somebody's psychic, Lol. I hope to live near him one day, he's a good guy.

Deep down in my gut I have a feeling that my brother's sabotage is worse than mine. He told me that he had his own place and a job when he first got there. (He lost his job and never got back on his feet-"he didn't say this to me"-it's just plain to see). He can't work either. (Unfortunately he wasn't keeping in touch with me enough for me to know that his situation had become dire). It's probably because people are harassing him about his sister being a ho. Which I'm not. He has switched rolls with his girlfriend. She works while he stays at home. Sounds like my current life to a 'T'. Well, not to a 'T' cause I'm single. But my daughter thinks she's in the parent roll, because she's working and I'm not. I'm quite sure that no matter where my brother lived; Maryland or Florida; he would not have been able to pan-handle like I'm doing without being beaten by the cops. (When I hadn't heard from him, I went looking for him). I'm a woman and I found myself toe to toe with men who carry guns, (cops); a few times. I guess he and I both are the designated homeless. It's funny because they all think we're jealous of them, (family and friends). Why would everyone be so mean to me and my brother?

I recall flying down to my uncles because we hadn't heard from my brother. I asked my uncle to drive me to Miami. I found my brother in a shelter. He drove back to Melbourne with us. I figured he would be OK from that day forward. By the time I got back home, I understand that he ended up back to Miami. I tried to help. I was living with my parents then. We have all really let my brother down. He was never a menace to society either. (Was I the one who'd found someone who didn't have anything and put em' off on family; family that now live in Newport?) – *Soul Food*. It is a relatively old movie. It would have to be some deep, deep sabotage to try to make scenes from **this movie**; come true. You and I both know, I would never be drinking to get drunk (I don't drink beer) and I would never go after someone else's husband; especially in their home. I don't drink beer. They wanted it to come true so badly, that their husband comes after me. Me and my daughter became homeless because I lost my job. You should never have forced me to move up there.

If I was the person they say. I would be rich from "ho-ing" or stripping. I am not a ho now, nor did I used to be. I just found out what "tricking" meant not too long ago.

OK I know he doesn't consider himself homeless anymore. He found love. I guess homelessness is a little different for military veterans. I hope so.

He loves his family. My brother was never violent in school or in our home. I've visited him several times and even tried to relocate once. I just didn't have the means or the money to do so. I love him. I truly miss him. I hope to live near him one day. He never joined any sports programs or joined any organizations in grade school but he is a very smart, kind person. I failed to mention that I cried all the way home after visiting him in 2004. I did not want to leave him.

Our Christmas' were grand. My mother was a giver. During the earlier part of the year, my brother used to always say something and then say sike. So one Christmas, I got a little box and wrapped it just for him. The only thing it contained was a note stating the word, sike. We all cracked up laughing. (His son sort of reminds you of the guy in the TV show Psyche). And the big brother's T-shirt has nothing but the word sike on the front in the movie- *Diary of a Wimpy Kid*. He and I got along for the most part. We definitely didn't fight like the two boys in this series of movies. Although he didn't used to be the best driver; that is definitely not him in Diary of a Wimpy Kid. He purchased a used old-timer car; you know the thick heavy kind. Unfortunately the brakes gave out and he ran into a police car. (Columbiana). That sounds like a very big ticket to me. If you can't pay your ticket they revoke your license. If you have no license, you have no job. I guess you have to use your personal documents to get a personal identification card. Which may not be as easy as it sounds. But still probably looks bad to an employer. I'm sure this was just the beginning of his problems.

I'm glad that my brother's son had such a fun and rewarding experience in grade school but it breaks my heart to know that my brother wasn't able to be a part of it. Anyone in a position to change his situation, should have. You can't get those precious moments back. Maybe they'll be closer now that his son is older and able to drive himself around.

I'm saddened to think that I can't get the time back that I've lost being so far away from my brother but I can only pray that we will see each other again and be able to enjoy each other's company for however long we have.

Some time ago I began a Small Business Management course at the local community college. I decided not to continue the class but forgot to drop the course. I simply walked away. I unknowingly acquired an 'E' on my transcript instead of what would have been an 'I' for Incomplete.

I took time to go back to graduate school in order to try to reboot myself. I chose a historically Black college to take my graduate level Education courses. Bowie state to be exact. I learned a lot but unfortunately the only class I really enjoyed was the class where the professor was White. But not before driving myself up to Columbia University to speak directly with an advisor about the Master of Journalism program. Although I never became a Broadcast Journalist, *Vantage Point* makes me sort of glad that I didn't. At least not somewhere dealing with political conflict. An actor/actress using my name is being blown-up while reporting. Maybe I can write stories for a newspaper or magazine, from 'home', Lol. I am now writing. I hope to write a few articles and books.

It's 1976 and I am 3 years old. The name of the Steakhouse has changed and our mothers were very close before mine passed away a little over 10 years ago. My middle name is her first name and our profiles are similar. I pray that neither one of our ships are sinking as on April 14, 1912. Although I'm the single parent, that's her mother's name. Her daughter is the one who is hard to impress in the movie Titanic. Is it September 11, 1792? Well, I'm not married. I hope she is.

I'm not feeling very lucky anymore, but I know I'm blessed.

Although my father 'warned' me that I would lose everything one day soon, ten years ago; (I have no idea why he would say that or allow it to happen); I wasn't expecting to be verbally harassed through my TV set where I live. I'm being threatened and harassed. Whoever it is, is saying that they warned me. I am not paranoid or crazy. I am not hearing things. I know my father isn't speaking to me through my TV. My father is still driving up from NC quite often. Although I am very hurt that I am being forced to live here without any money; I am trying my best to walk in the love of God with my immediate family. This day, I need the $25 to renew my cosmetology license. There is now a $25 late fee. Is this another something that I'm about to lose?

www.ingramcontent.com/pod-product-compliance
Lightning Source LLC
Chambersburg PA
CBHW030524290526
45786CB00004B/1609